Poems of The Mad Hunter

and other tales

BYRON HOOT

"The North Country is a place

outside and inside us.

Make no mistake about that."

Poems of The Mad Hunter and other tales

Publication facilitated by Forest River initiatives, LLC

d/b/a Quimby, Pickford and Cheshire Publishers

Hoot/Byron, G. 10/9/2022

ISBN: 9798363051968

First Edition: November 15, 2022

This book is the ninth book of poetry from the author. Other books by Byron Hoot include: *The Art of Grilling, Monster in The Kingdom, In Our Time, Such Beautiful Sense, These Need No Title, Poems from the Woods & Piercing the Veil.*

Cover Art: **Field Point** (front) & **King of The North Country** (back) from stylized photos sourced by the author edited using Varnist ® software. All artworks in this book are stylized photographs using Varnist ®.

Foreword

In *The Great Gatsby*, narrator Nick Carraway opines that
there is no difference between people "so profound as the
difference between the sick and the well." It's a phrasing
too delicious not to want to apply to all manner of
situations. Between people who read and people who
don't, for instance. (I think Mark Twain said that). Or:
there is no difference so profound as that between those
who hunt and those who do not.

To be clear, I am of the latter group. I grew up on the
South Shore of Boston, and although we spent many
hours casting lines on fresh and salt water, my family did
not hunt in the traditional sense. This is not to say that
hunting wasn't an option; there was abundant wild game,
including some that's almost never seen there now. In my
youth it was common to be startled as a Ring-necked
Pheasant burst from field cover and flapped swiftly away.
Ironically, these birds, which are native to Asia, were
holdovers in New England from days when wealthy
sportsmen imported them to private estates for hunting.
The Wild Turkey, on the other hand, very much native to
those parts, was virtually unknown. These days a
pheasant would be a rarity, while turkeys wander in
placid abundance on suburban lawns. As I write this, out

my window several large crows are in a noisy standoff with a larger red-tailed hawk.

My presence in the "non-hunting" camp likely owes to not having been exposed to the hunt growing up more than from some ethical resistance. That being said, no one has opened up the world of the hunter for me as expressively, as illuminatingly, and yes, as beautifully, as Byron Hoot. Over the five decades since we first met (as fellow gym rats and aspiring writers, at Eastern Nazarene College) and became friends, he has shown an enduring passion for hunting—and a yen to share that.

Hoot comes to this by birthright. Born and raised in the Appalachia of West Virginia and North Central Pennsylvania, he has ancestral roots in the hunt. A grandfather, an uncle, and cousins were his first guides. While his father didn't hunt in the usual sense, he did so metaphorically as a Nazarene preacher. Given this lineage (which he traces in the poem "Hunters") Hoot, served his apprenticeship in the woods and learned to be, like most hunters, a steward of the forest and its wildlife. These he observes with a tender and clear-eyed regard. It is this particularity, the level of observational detail, which makes his work intensely present.

His poems throb with the pulse of Nature, a concept he often renders simply as the "North Country" or "North Woods" – a synecdoche denoting all wilderness. His concerns are with an awareness of topography and terrain, of biology and meteorology, of sensory input. He is deeply interested in sign and spoor and trails and, yes, the link between hunter and quarry. Interestingly, the "hardware" of hunting (weapons and gear; what Faulkner might designate the "lifeless mechanicals") is near-to-invisible in these poems. This could owe to his being a hunter writing for hunters, but the evidence of the poems and his own statements ("Everyone,/ I have decided, is a hunter …") signal a larger embrace.

The phrase "Mad Hunter," is humorous, allusive, and a marker that it's the interior of mind and hunt he is concerned with. The poetic voice is intimately linked with hunting's history and its destiny. Hoot is keyed to a dimension of soul, wherein alertness, courage, humility, compassion, have primacy. It isn't a stretch to draw comparisons with such spirit hunters as Black Elk, Faulkner, Wendell Berry (who Hoot quotes as a source for his title), Jim Harrison, Edward Hoagland, Louise Erdrich, Barry Lopez, and others, some of whose hunting was done only with the eyes. In addition to being an adept at hunting and the woods, Hoot is devout student of literature. A writer most certainly invoked is Thoreau. "Many men go fishing all of their lives," he wrote, "without knowing that it is not fish they are after." One could add an "only" before "fish."

Hoot shows his hand in varied ways: "there is a something that wants to keep me/ in the woods…" he writes in "Tricks of the Wind." And: "It is an ancient religion/ this hunting, and deer an old God" in "God is a White-tailed Deer"

Quirky, solitary, idiosyncratic, Hoot's voice on the page is insistently original. In ways, his diction is nearer to Faulkner than to any poet. His work can be frustrating at times, too, when rendered in syntactical units that bump against the sense of the lines. However, the tension between crystalline clarity and ambiguity requires a reader to be alert—like a hunter.

There's an attitude of attention. "I sit, catching my breath and listen." ["Catch My Breath and Listen"]

And an honoring of what is, that can come through in haiku-like compression:

"I see the remnants of a spider web/catching snow" ["Caught in the Illusion"]

While maintaining watchful focus, the hunter sometimes achieves a kind of Zen no-mind. In the poem "Lost in Falling Snow" the observer reflects: "I'm here to hunt/ and not to lose myself in this falling snow./ Still,/ this hillside, this tree stand, me,/ the tracks below, the runway crossing/ just beyond the fallen tree, and this moment/ are all snow falling from the sky."

One of my names for Byron Hoot is "Bear Claw" – a jocular, affectionate nod at Will Geer's character in Jeremiah Johnson. It would not be a stretch to consider any number of animals as Hoot's totems: bear, deer, wild turkey, wolf. And there's the large tattoo of an owl (one almost expects it to wink) on the poet's shoulder. The play on his name is clear, and fun, and there is the association of wisdom, which Hoot possesses.

What Byron Hoot brings to the great North Country is wisdom earned through his efforts and time at task—and at the same time, as though in beneficence for his attention, it's as though the forest bestowed upon him some form of sanctification. And it may be this he is most eager to share in these poems. But he has no evangelical bent; he is not seeking to make converts. He is lighting out for the territories and taking us with him. For this reason, when entering the poems—and the woods—one does well to bring an attitude of openness, wonder, and respect.

David Daniel / October 2022

Introduction

This volume of poems began as a single book, not three.

The original intent was for Poems of the Mad Hunter to be a solo work. A series of bombastic, tall-tale type poems about life through the experience of hunting. Like Walden Pond meets Field & Stream with a Paul Bunyan persona. An idea inspired by Wendell Barry.

Then I said to my editor, "I also have a chapbook called 'Meditations from a Tree stand'. Would you like to see that?"

"Yes," and after reading it he said, "You write hunting poems during the season, don't you? Dig up eight or ten of those for me and let's think about this."

I did and now, somehow, we have a triptych of sorts.

The first part is the meditations; the second the proclamations, the third – Reading Sign – the considerations.

They're all about hunting and they're not at all about hunting.

The details of the poems lead far beyond the taking of a deer, which all true hunting does. It leads beyond the borders and boundaries into and through oneself, leads to a deeper understanding of who we are. Of what Nature IS. Not the call of but *to* the wild that we recognize as something good, something undeniable.

If we want to be civilized, we need to love the wilds, the natural sanctuary of woods and streams, the liturgy of wildlife, game for a hunter, a preparation that makes us ready when time and eternity meet in the split second of an unforgettable moment.

And not deny the affects. . ..

And so, what we have is my editor's coaction of combining three books of poetry into one representing over forty hunting seasons and a lifetime of hunting stories, antlers, and bear sign. It represents the dreams of youth, the practice and patience of maturity. It's four decades of reading and learning and bearing all kinds of weather, of getting lost and finding my way back home.

All these years of hunting and I'm still finding my way back to who I am. The self is the hunt that never ends.

I hope you find these poems speak to you.

~ B.H.

Dedication

These meditations, mad poems and sign readings are dedicated to the memory of my grandfather, Byron Holt Mead and my uncle, Ted P. Heckathorn, who lived the question — What's life?

To them, I owe my love of the hunt and the woods and of course, the stillness.

*

Stillness in The North Country

There is nothing like the stillness of the woods;

neither wind nor bird nor animal breaking

the wait for nothing to join the stillness

and dance.

Leading and following the same thing.

I worry my breath and heart and blood

disrupt the moment

but I am here like a hermit seeing what I can't speak

and hold my bow.

Poems of The Mad Hunter and other tales

Table of Contents

BOOK ONE: Meditations from a Tree Stand

Thoughts on The Meditations

These meditations represent the hunting season, but I often find I have the same thoughts and feelings in the same place year after year. There are only certain things that you can see and feel when you're hunting. Some thoughts that occur out in the woods never occur when you're in the office, in the plant, on the road or at home. And despite all the new technology that aids us in getting to be better hunters, it's still you, the game, the land, and what you do when the moment of truth comes: no amount of technology will change that. When we get ready for hunting season something very old enters us.

There is something in hunting that makes all clocks seem ridiculous, all our civilized ways suspect, and what we do for a living — ludicrous.

These meditations explore some of these matters. There's an ambiguity hunting makes us feel. And yes, there is always something disquieting about taking an animal's life that meditation can never overcome.

I hope you enjoy these meditations.

What Will I Remember?

What will I dream about?

The last shot of the day,

the season, at 4:00 o'clock

when three deer came out of the sun

across the top of the hill

heading towards a tree stand

I had found.

They came and stopped,

then moved,

taking them out of the sunlight,

put them more into it.

I drew on the first

but the last one started to raise her tail

move her ears and stomp

I shot.

Too soon!

Stayed still,

but could not reload

fast enough.

They walked away

across the upper bowl of the valley.

I never hunt without

learning something.

I have already

dreamed and seen

that scene a dozen times —

it will stay with me until next season

to see

if I will know any more then

than I did the other day

the last day

the last shot

when deer walked away.

Catch My Breath and Listen

I walk up the hill to the first shelf

where the tree stand is.

By the time I reach it,

I have unzipped my coat.

I climb up and sit, zip my coat back up.

I am at eye level if the deer come over the hill,

but well above them

if they come around the hill.

Still, I cannot see everything,

and must move to see behind me.

Every advantage has a disadvantage.

I sit, catch my breath and listen.

Tricks of The Wind

When I get ready to leave the woods,

I suddenly hear footsteps

that freeze me

and I slowly turn my ear

to where the sound is.

It is nothing

but the wind in the leaves or in the top of the trees,

my willingness to be deceived.

I stop and listen. I know better.

Having refused the tricks of the wind

all day.

Yet now, with the beginning of dusk

I think the trick real.

There is something that wants to keep me

in the woods, some whisper promising

just the right shot in the last light of day

if I stay a little longer . . . I say, "No,"

and walk out of the woods in darkness.

Some Order of Things

There is some order

to the way these trees have grown,

have fallen, some order

to where the deer come from and go,

when they come and go,

to this

desire to hunt.

I know my ignorance pushes

my intelligence beyond my knowledge.

There is something like that

being in the woods hunting deer,

some wild assurance

this is what I need to do,

some order of things I am in

that does not make sense

to everyone.

Listening to What Nothing Means

It took me a long time to learn

when to move to sound and when not to.

When I first hunted

I thought every sound was the footstep

of a deer.

Now, I know better. There is the top branch

and the low ground wind sound, squirrels,

chipmunks, birds, turkeys barking and calling.

There is only the sound of clothes against branches,

underbrush to betray me as I move.

It takes a long time to learn these sounds

and to know the footsteps of deer in leaves,

snapping a twig, smelling the air, snorting, stomping

their hooves. Sometimes at the end of the day

I grow ignorant again hoping for more deer,

one more shot, one more story, one more gift

granted by the gods of the hunt.

Listening to what nothing means.

The Last Temptation

I remember the kiss to Michelle's neck

last night before I went downstairs

and how her top cut into a V.

I slowly turn to see what it is behind me,

but instead see her stepping out

of the shower the second before

she wraps the towel around her body.

My feet are getting cold, as are my hands.

The snow is falling. There is no wind.

It is cold and our bed,

I know, is warm

and I am beginning to wonder

what I am doing here after all.

Caught in the Illusion

It is late in the season, five days left.

There is a certain

relief to the ending.

I am rutted down by the hunt;

now, I see one, two, maybe three deer.

And still, I cannot stop planning

and hunting.

I see the remnants of a spider web

catching snow,

see how the slightest breeze

casts an illusion of the moment,

snow caught on a spider's web

in winter.

The Unsettling

I have decided to talk only to hunters.

Everyone,

I have decided, is a hunter, even those who say

they could never hunt tell me how they see

so many deer and turkey, how they love

the beauty of the woods, the sky at twilight.

There is one thing in us,

something deep that pulls us

to the woods,

that gives us a hunter's vision —

This cannot be denied!

I smile.

There are times I have to talk about it,

embarrassing myself

and those listening

the way Jehovah's Witnesses

unsettle you

when they come to the door.

Signs on the Landscape of My Heart

I hunt the seasons, but I am a hunter

the way I am a husband, father, son,

brother, grandson, uncle,

nephew, cousin.

When I hunt, I see Michelle and our children.

I see my parents—

Once, hunting bear, I saw my mother

in the woods waiting for me at a tree

along with my grandparents, all ghosts now.

When I am home, I see deer appearing

in the corners of our rooms, tracks across the carpet.

I sit in this tree stand

and look out across the hillside; inside,

I am roaming the landscape of my heart,

sometimes its wilderness.

There is so much hunting to be done,

it will take a lifetime to know

how to read the sign just right.

Lost in Falling Snow

The snow falls.

What does it feel like

to be snow?

I'm here to hunt

and not to lose myself in this falling snow.

Still,

this hillside, this tree stand, me,

the tracks below, the runway crossing

just beyond the fallen tree,

and this moment

are all snow falling from the sky.

God is a White-tailed Deer

I think God is a white-tailed deer

leaving split hooved marks

near and clear enough to draw us

to the woods, to the trails that wind

and climb disappearing in a stand

of pines, to places we've never been before.

It is an ancient religion

this hunting, and deer an old God.

The desire in me

takes me to a place where I cannot tell

the difference between the deer and me.

There is a hunter

in everyone following a trail that promises

a moment when everything is just right.

The way God was just right for Moses

in a burning bush or on Mount Sinai.

Look!

The sign is right before your eyes!

BOOK TWO: Poems of The Mad Hunter

Reflections on The Mad Hunter

Somewhere around 2010 I bought Wendell Berry's *The Mad Farmer Poems. Poems of the Mad Hunter* tries to maintain that singular tone and sense of Berry's *Mad Farmer*.

That sense is mainly of frustration with a life given over to an economy of built-in obsolesce, of believing any progress is better than no progress, of accepting the authority of corporations and corporations' fraternal twin — government.

The Mad Hunter attempts a return to silence and away from the cacophony of a noisy, intrusive chatter and continuous advertisements of what I can only imagine hell is like. There's also a conscious act of turning away from ourselves under a banner of becoming who we truly are.

The Mad Hunter therefore agrees with the *Mad Farmer*. They are a similar breed seeing many of the same things from a slightly different perspective.

Now, I'm no farmer but I do have a love of the land. A love fostered by growing up in the hills of West Virginia. Of going off by myself beginning when I was eight "to the woods," climbing fences, crossing fields with cattle in them. Entering the woods. Fishing ponds. Returning midday or early evening. Yes, I knew instinctively where I belonged.

Some four hours away, in north central Pennsylvania, my grandparents and aunt and uncle lived. At Thanksgiving and Christmas, we'd make the drive to be with Mom's family. And there, I heard the stories of deer and bear hunts. Hunted rabbits Thanksgiving mornings. Spent summers there where the woods held only wild game, logging roads, and deer trails.

The stories lingered for a long time until I started to tell mine. I can't imagine my life without hunting seasons.

These poems, like Berry's, have a character larger than life. Exaggerated language. Opinions easy and hard to swallow. The persona of *The Mad Hunter* is a composite creation of a tall tale character who slashes and cuts to get to the core of things in hunting and life. These poems are not so much in praise of hunting but a consideration. Some may offend. Some may be troubling. All are spoken by a Mad Hunter engaged in that eternal question – What's life?

Fear

I fear my grandchildren are beyond

the redemption of the hunt.

Which worries me.

They may never know the primal truths

that hone a soul to be a man –

hard enough but more so when removed from trees

and hills and stream, learning game,

reading sign.

All necessary to being better today than yesterday.

Lessons that can be taken in.

I hunt and fish religiously.

In ways sacred, where knowing and honoring

and deciding in a split-second matter

as the metaphysical realities they are.

Metaphors full of meaning, the wilds give

what no cities can. I worry what kind of stories

my grandsons will tell sitting around a fire.

Hunters

Not everyone is born to go into the woods.

I was,

though not through a father who hunted,

but born from my grandfather and uncle

and cousin and my aunt's boyfriend –

I trace my lineage.

To walk into the woods is to enter

a different dimension of time and space

and acts and feelings and thoughts –

if thought

it can be called.

There is to be found things

about yourself that the sounds of traffic

and conversation

will never reveal.

You know if the woods are for you

and you for the woods

the first time you step in.

When I was a kid

I was nicknamed

Tonto – I already knew then

where I belonged, making bows from maples,

arrows from cattails, carved wooden

arrowheads, and fletching

found from fallen bird feathers.

When I was fifty-eight

someone I hunt with called me Tonto.

You can't escape the essence of who you are;

I told the story of that nickname –

we took two deer that day.

When we meet for breakfast,

we are looked upon with fear and desire

as if we were some lost tribe stumbling into

civilization: they took our money just the same

and we left knowing we were marked men

carrying some of the dreams from the eyes

that watched us leave.

The Birthright

You're born to it.

Can't argue anyone to enter the woods

the way arguments can persuade someone

to do what they don't want to

because the money's good.

Not that *that* logic never works in the long run,

but it certainly doesn't work

if the hunt isn't in your blood.

It's often the hunt that counterbalances

that argument where money wins

and your soul shudders with each day.

Being told to follow an economic dream

that is no dream at all.

Love and family and the way things are

and the way men are, I mean the way they can do

what is not in them to do and do it well

and refuse the pain of unfulfilled dreams

that the hunt is the antidote for.

The hunt makes the scar of their soul

not ache but is a place

from which they constantly dream and do not mind

body aches or missing the chance

to make another day's pay because they are

doing what they dream and need to do.

Many maintain that balance

with a stubborn bear hug grip.

This time we live is not very good

at matching our avocations and vocations,

as two eyes seeing one vision

our needs and dreams joining

in some long ago vision this age refuses

to acknowledge.

The farther we are from the woods,

the further we are from our hearts –

deep down that is always

understood.

Time Matters

Time goes beyond schedules and deadlines

in the woods.

There, time and place hold each other

with no sense of urgency,

no sense of right or wrong

because if you've done your scouting

you're where you are, enough sign has drawn you.

Now you wait like some prophet waiting

to hear God speak.

All eyes and ears and a sixth sense

that takes a long time to get

lets you slowly turn your head

to see what you first sensed

before you saw anything.

Down below, time and place don't congregate

like that and thinking in A, B, C logic falls away

like old snakeskin up here.

There is more,

more than the mind wants

to acknowledge is known by no mind at all

up north in the woods —

hunting the whole history

of mankind in your blood

not just the latest gadgetry

of the newest technology

that takes you further from yourself and others.

Sometimes the deer appear; sometimes they don't.

That's a fact

of which both statements are guarantees.

Let some *desk rider* in an office hold two facts

like that and be satisfied with the time

and place he finds himself in

and the walk out of the woods with

or without a deer equally satisfying –

not likely. It's just that time and place

mean so differently up north.

"The kingdom is among you," Jesus said;

up there, we all know what that means.

We Know

There are men and women

who do not miss the grace of first light,

the seductive sigh of dusk,

who feel the land and trees

and sky as well as they see what moves and flies

across their eyes,

who tell stories, draw characters

in detail, often end with some

common sense benediction they're not

afraid to utter nor are others

embarrassed to agree.

They use language unfit for church

but do not feel hypocritical though

the sanctuary and love of the woods

makes a church pew hardly bearable.

In groups or singularly we all lumber

into the woods as quietly as we can

in pre-dawn light knowing

the essence of hunting –

mixed with all we know –

is basically ambush, being ready without knowing

when the moment

will be right.

Down below, any

refusal to know

confuses the work world when

an answer is sought; "We'll see"

are the only words to be uttered,

understood only in their exact patience

in the woods . . .

When language is caught

in acts words crumble,

and every hunter I know has this silent

vocabulary full of meaning

that unnerves those whose words

are full of definitions and their acts empty.

I have never known

a hunter who did not have a sense of beauty,

a love for Nature;

no, redneck, hicks are terms

that do not matter.

You can never carry

words like that into the woods

where every tree and stream and bird

and animal and sky and breeze

and hunter fit exactly where they are.

The Keepers

It's true: we wear shirts and ties,

punch clocks, take salaries,

go to church, cut grass, do chores.

But we are keepers of something

as old as mankind –

the simple union

of man with woods

and the hunt, which has been

denigrated and dignified –

neither one exactly true

as the essence of hunting

is neither too little nor too much,

letting thought go only so far,

letting intuition lead but not blindly:

it is the state of "is completely,"

the moment whole,

the time fulfilled,

expectations that do not exclude anything –

this is what we hold and love to offer

and has always been held by those who hunt.

This brotherhood began

when man began

and knows nothing of race or gender

or politics or boundaries

and is understood in every tongue

where hunting stories are told.

It is a stream against the stream

that wants to wash all our humanity away . . .

hunting,

the first act that struck the chord

sounding our humanity.

Return

The farther we have left the woods behind

the less human we have become.

To be civilized does not mean

we have become more human.

There are some things we do

that call up primeval truths

that are deep in us

and need to be heard,

repeated, chanted, worked

into the blood by following a trail

through the woods, waking before dawn,

falling asleep to only the sounds

of night –

no phones, no radio, no TV . . .

nothing that gives that false sense of receiving,

shaping our perceptions by what

is manufactured for convenience

and entertainment's sake.

To touch the ground

is to touch heaven; the kingdom is here

and always has been and to shake

the earth off our souls is to disgrace

the universe.

Those heaven chasers

are just as brutally civilized

as those city dwellers who trust only

to their own fantasies disregarding

the source of imagination and reality –

all of Nature in her splendor

and terror.

That's how our stories are minted,

how our hearts are made,

how our faces and bodies and hearts

and souls are etched

with divine and human combined.

Let churches rot!

Let the Bibles be burned!

Let scripture be rewritten!

Rewritten from Nature, God's first mistress,

first truth-sayer, most faithful lover

of all given to us as to God.

Return to the woods; *return to yourself* –

your soul longs for Nature

outside and in

at once.

The Force that Flows

There is some force that flows

through tree and hill and stream and deer

and bear and turkey and small

game and birds and fishes

that is beyond anything we can

explain though cannot deny.

Every hunter knows this.

It is in their blood before the woods

confirm that truth of their existence

they may never utter but never deny.

Too much steel and concrete

and right angles lets a man think

he's someone he isn't,

the mind something it isn't

and time and meaning something marked,

clearly defined – it isn't.

Nothing so conspires towards our humanity

as feet touching ground, as tracking game,

reading sign,

being under an open sky and far away

from any inside, except the one the heart

opens up inside you . . .

that infinite grace of being alive

just where you are with nothing else

that can be done except what you're doing:

try that down below, out of the North country

and you'll see just how small you've become

by constraints which do not free

but bind you

to someone else's image

of whom you are to be!

The soul needs a broad expanse of country

to wonder in – every hunter knows that,

knows salvation isn't done by committee

but by being in the presence of those

who are who they are and need no one

to tell them they are saved or damned,

words that mean nothing once

"I am that I am," is uttered

in some deep wood hunting

heard by no one but known by all

who have uttered those five words before.

Get your feet onto the ground,

your eyes scanning in front of

and out beyond,

your ears attuned to the sounds of the woods,

decide what type of hunter you are –

you just have one life to live.

Too Much Not So

I can tell you what is wrong with us.

It is no economic matter,

but a matter of the soul,

the distance we've removed ourselves from Nature,

from doing what we want and having so many

needs that are not our desires, our dreams,

our choices cannot satisfy.

Curse all advertising

and their claim creating markets for products

we can live without.

You think the reason

people shy away from hunters

is because we hunt?

It's because we are not afraid to be who we are

And the truths we hold as self-evident

are as old as mankind

and that ruffles the feathers of those

who only hold what has recently been minted

passing for silver and gold

when it isn't.

Our presence says we are apart

from the common lot of humanity.

We are of the oldest,

truest form of humanity:

when you pursue game in Nature

you learn a lot about yourself.

We are a revolution of one

and quietly move

through this world hearing, "Be who you are,

you'll get what you need."

Any fool can look at a tree or a deer

and see how true these words are.

Not Everyone Is

I know many hunters I would not hunt with.

Because a person hunts

doesn't mean they're a hunter.

I've known many killers in the woods

who only see the hunt as an escape,

a play of "*once upon a time*,"

a time to show their skill of marksmanship,

but who are not satisfied without a kill.

I stay away from them

and hope they change.

They're not much for the beauty of the woods,

what Nature wants to teach,

not satisfied with a long day's hunt

that ends in praise of deer

who outsmarted us with skills

we keep seeking to possess.

No, it isn't always true

a hunter is a hunter is a hunter.

There's sorrow in having to admit that,

a certain rage that tinges the edge of that truth,

but that's the way it is.

All are not called to be hunters.

Still,

there are enough who love the hunt

in all its aspects to keep the world aright,

much, I suppose, the way monks and nuns pray

without the world knowing

the value of those unheard prayers

but faithfully uttered for everyone alive.

I think the hunt is prayer

and does more good than we know

if we are hunters

learning about Nature

outside and in.

Open Season

Hunting isn't about a season,

it's about a state of the heart that is there

day-in, day-out and never disappears

even when you can't enter the woods anymore.

I sit now in late summer

watching leaves and grass,

feeling the layers in the air –

some now slightly cool –

watch the pelage of the deer slowly change,

the color of their coats, sure sign

of the passing of the year in some other sense

of time whose beginning is not every January.

Looking and listening

for the yet to be seen,

reading the sign

left to guide us to them

carries over when we're back to the world of work

and hours and weeks and bosses

and those who are unnerved by the smell

and presence of the wild we have

that will not, cannot be denied.

Once you start seeing things through a hunter's eye

you never see things the same way you once did.

It's true with the listening as well

not to mention that other sense

that comes on you and guides you

to look twice or three times and see what wasn't

is now quietly, suddenly there.

You don't leave any of this back at camp,

in the woods.

it becomes part of who you are,

and it threatens those who have forgotten it,

who have bowed to dreams and desires not theirs,

who have refused their right of refusal.

A Hunting Lesson

The shortest thing about hunting is the killing;

it's the hunt that elongates time and depth

and width and the height of every moment

in the woods the soul longs for.

Of course, you take the game when it appears

to honor it and the hunt

and all you've learned to that point.

When you leave the woods

it's in your blood and never stops flowing:

"You are who you are

and you're not who you're not."

It's pretty simple

and those who are who they are not

are always uncomfortable around those

who are who they are.

When you're a hunter you know the heart

is about more than what appears –

what you learn works into the creases

on your hands, on your face,

into your muscle, blood, and bone

and unnerves those who never learn

how to taste the wind,

see into the woods,

work the dirt out from underneath fingernails,

sit in a circle of hunters

around a fire telling stories,

drinking beer.

The Difference

Shooting, practiced long enough,

turns into an art.

It is not an art at first. It demands a discipline

that will not be forgone, stepped aside,

if there is not hunter blood

running through your veins.

I know something of art

and what is true of it –

integrity, harmony, clarity –

is true of shooting too.

Not just shooting but taking the shot.

There's time the moment only almost combines

to let the shot be made.

Every hunter I know has passed on game

because the shot wasn't there –

to make that judgment is to go beyond skill,

to enter the realm of art where everything fits.

It's a movable moment in the hunt

and those moments are never exactly alike.

That essence is taken out of the woods,

back to villages and towns and cities

and farms: each moment holding the

integrity and harmony and clarity

that only it can give and only you can receive,

(*that being where you are completely*).

The great advantage of the woods

is that you can't be any place else and be hunting,

even in a group you primarily hunt alone.

When you know whether to make the shot

your skill and experiences

have turned into art.

Everything comes together

for a split second of eternity.

Some hunters are skilled, some are masters . . .

it's not hard

to know the difference.

And What Is Gained?

I have yet to see how all the technology

that is to give us more time compares

to the time between sunrise and sunset.

Out in the woods, time there

elongates the way a deer does when

it jumps through the air.

I see a certain, corporate-shackled slavery

in cellphone and computers

and the avenues of instant access

and the false sense of doing more

without doing it better.

Just because you can be in greater contact

does not mean depth of the touch has grown.

And the sense of always being *"on call,"*

that annoying habit of constantly checking phones

in the presence of another, texting, talking

while another person (who is present)

is usurped by someone who is not present —

disgusts me.

Most places I hunt a cell phone or computer

won't even work —

a benefit of an unknown yet incalculable

degree of magnitude the soul craves *and receives*.

Even God knows the value of being out of touch,

especially from those moments we cry,

"Why have You forsaken ME?"

and resurrection is His reply.

The presence of other hunters,

of woods and sign and game and moments

which may or may not come

and told around a campfire eating and drinking

at the end of the day

is enough to satisfy the soul

and it is the soul's satisfaction

we should concern ourselves with,

its needs and its dreams and its desires.

Our purpose is not to be accessible but to touch

and be touched, to be where we are

with who is beside us.

This is not taught but known, passed on in story,

and those who have ears hear, those with eyes see;

this simplicity of sight and sound abounds

but cannot be found, often, where we are.

But go to the woods to find your soul

become a hunter, a tracker

a reader of sign

and soon – ten maybe fifteen years –

you'll find you can read both outer and inner sign

equally well.

No technology can teach you the art of the heart

the way the woods can

when you enter as a hunter and die

finally, as a man, a woman,

a human being

heaven and earth created for us

to be as we are meant to be.

A Moment's Hesitation

I hesitate to call hunters, *hunters,*

the same way I hesitate to call myself

by some political party, or Christian or sinner. . .

It is the naming of things properly that matters most

and it is that very tendency that leads –

once so named – to no change in us

and we end up defending the indefensible,

refusing changes as natural as the season

for a consistency of which there is only one eternity

– change.

So, while I proclaim the virtue of the hunter,

the values of the hunter,

each of us knows the value of going our own way,

the danger of a group too strongly identified with

and how sometimes you have to say, "No"

to that which has brought you to where you are

in order to go further, learn more,

and not get caught by what you know

when every season teaches something new,

gives something never before given.

To be a hunter is not like joining a church.

It is more like repeating after God who did not say

"I am God," but said only,

"I will be as I will be," and that was enough

and that is enough for me

though I think, *believe*, know if the hunt

is in you these six words come alive.

I say there is virtue in the hunt,

value in the hunter

no more.

Beyond Dispute

The woods and streams,

fish and animals and birds

are never untrue to themselves.

Of course, that's no guarantee being

in their presence

rubs off –

sometimes it doesn't,

sometimes it does.

At least we're given

to be among those who are

never untrue

to whom they are.

My Only

. . .cry against technology

is we use it to distance ourselves from ourselves

and others and then pretend we don't.

I had ordered a pizza and ran into a husband

and wife I had not seen for some time.

Both shook my hand and then turned their heads

down to their texting.

"We"

were there in a moment, but not really.

When you sit around a fire at the end of a day's hunt

there's no texting.

There is conversation, slow, and rambling,

the stories of the day, the plans for tomorrow.

At least when we're in Nature we get a chance,

at least a chance,

to be who we were born to be,

I mean to see and to hear

and to know and to act and to have

that sixth sense about reality

that makes us turn for no reason at all

to let us see what would have gone unseen –

it's hard

to see like that when your vision

is restricted to a system with limited possibilities. . .

unlike hunting

where the possible is limitless

both inwardly and outwardly,

the two as one simultaneously.

The Call

These late summer rains

weaken the leaf to its limb,

not to mention the wind's twisting and bending

of trees and branches, ripping of leaves.

I am sitting down below

far from the North Country

to which I will soon go.

Nature doesn't know that though;

what is true here is true there –

the rains, the wind, the heaviness of summer's green

now almost too much to keep . . .

I see new housing plans being cut into hillsides

and inwardly weep

at the graded streets, the numbered lots,

the remnants of trees left to represent

the beauty the hillside once held fully sacred.

You cannot throw the wilderness away

discard it like some out-of-date appliance.

Nature dreams in hundreds-of-hundreds of years

to be as it is to be

and in a week's wreckage

the face of Nature changes.

We have never understood we are owned

by the land,

breathe and live because of it,

because of rain, because of sun,

because of day and night,

because of planting and harvesting,

because of hunting and fishing,

because we are a part of Nature

and not apart from her.

Nothing is truer than this.

I Think

. . .of hunters and artists in the same way –

if what they do is done right there's hope

for everyone, even those who refuse the hunter

or the artist in themselves . . .

Each, however,

can see and hear and know what to do –

hunters and artists who are true

to the hunt and to the art

are the hope our future clings to.

BOOK THREE: Reading Sign

Insights on Reading Sign

We are all sign readers. Sign leavers. Sign seekers. Sign followers and we have always been. The preparation for the readiness of hunting, the willingness to go into the woods is not complete until the desire to read sign puts its mark on you.

Hoof prints, droppings, a rub, a scrape, a nibbled branch all *mean something*. And the willingness to follow where they lead often make expectations and previous knowledge something to be added to.

The turn of a trail takes you where you've never been.

Sometimes right to the deer. Sometimes close. Sometimes the sign disappears.

I think what it means to be alive and how hunting sharpens that realm in me to what I can come to know, how I come to know myself. How connected the obvious and hard to see are. How I, too, leave sign by words and acts for others whether I want to or not.

All of which is the essence of sign: leaving something behind that draws the heart and eye and body to follow.

And how to do so takes you to the edge of where you've never been. The way deer and the divine draw us to the edge of things to where we are meant to go if we just follow the sign leaving the wannabe hunters close to camp dreaming of what cannot be.

The sign leading to the edge of reality. The promised land just across the creek. The deer and the divine spiriting in and out of sight. And following the sign others may never see.

Ghosts Burning

Have I seen the deer in the woods

appear and disappear

to find out it was only a ghost

walking old trails feeding on memories?

And how many times have I seen

a ghost turn into a deer?

It happens.

So, I am not surprised by the story of Pentecost

where some saw the flame

about the head and some did not.

I draw the bow, release the arrow

and in a split second, sound and sight

confirm the strike or miss.

What's real is the burning flame,

the flying arrow of desire.

Waiting for Another Dream

The soul and heart wrestled with dreams.

Forgetting what that does, I awoke tired,

slow to go hunting, my desire dripping

like drops of water from a spigot

that can't be turned off.

I made coffee.

The evening before we had seen nearly fifty deer

feeding in fields,

along the road and knew what that meant —

a front was coming in.

They'd stay put in the morning.

We knew that.

The others got ready, but I lingered until I decided

why not?

We were hoping against the facts,

and that hope, like faith, would upend reality

with a deer and an arrow . . .

The wind blew making the leaves

sound like falling rain.

Walking back to camp I wondered

if my heart and soul had won

or if they were waiting for another dream.

The Pull of The Woods

How certain the pull of the woods on me.

Something in the blood understands

I do not try, have to remember, what I cannot forget.

I have no words to say just how this is,

only that when I see the uneven tree line,

a place where field and woods edge one another,

a trail I can see from the road

something happens in me.

Some recognition of who I am,

was born to be,

something enhancing who I am enters

and does not leave nor ever fills me completely –

my eyes and heart watching-watching,

seeing.

Forgiveness That Cannot be Refused

The two bucks were in the backyard

in a plan, in a suburb.

This happens all the time,

this call of the wild

calling to you and me.

The persistence

like forgiveness

that cannot be refused.

To Jacob

I used to think that taking deer

was the thing about hunting,

but somewhere my thinking changed

when I started to learn

what hunting was teaching.

I learned to study by doing

and reading what deer do and how

to read the sign,

learned to practice with bow and rifle

and shotgun, learned that so much

has to be just right for that shot –

which is a juxtaposition of time and place and me

and the deer to be aligned

in the flickering of an eye

before the moment's gone.

I learned to see, to be still,

learned to listen which eventually

led to no words in my head

distracting me from hearing

the crack of a twig revealing

what was coming into sight.

Mostly, I learned patience

and that judgments aren't always right.

That to be a hunter is a way of life

that goes far beyond any season.

The Patience of Waiting

I have taken the silence and stillness of the hunt

out of the woods with me.

The patience of waiting ingrained.

They may all be faults outside the realms of the wild.

Or virtues long forgotten

and not any longer known, and so.

Well and so.

I know I discard much I know when I go in;

there is another body of knowledge needed

just beyond the edges.

I think how many edges there are,

what to leave behind,

what to pick up,

mark my direction

and where I enter

in order to return.

The Suddenness of Being Known

I was listening for a twig to snap.

The ground was wet,

the leaves were wet,

silence abetting sight and intuition.

I sought the sound of a deer

betraying itself and knew

what I was listening for, knew the difference

between acorns dropping, a branch falling.

Knew, too, how silent dampness makes the woods,

hides scent, muffles even crow caws,

squirrel barking, birdsong.

Began to wonder how often

I had snapped a twig and revealed a part of me

I thought was nothing more than a step I had taken

as I meandered to where I was going

destination unknown

and then

the suddenness of being known.

Remembered I was hunting deer,

got lost in the koan –

isn't all hunting

hunting for yourself?

and turned my head to hear.

Talisman

I go to the woods for reasons

other than hunting, but if I wasn't hunting

the reasons wouldn't appear.

I see and hear the way an old song makes images

and feelings appear,

the ones that need no thinking

but are full of dreams and logic in subtle arguments

creating places where I go

I would not have gone.

And always the invitation,

"Take something back of me." Not a lot,

but a token of remembrance,

a talisman that may be useful, something

to call upon when the semblance of reality

bends like a tree ready to break.

I know what I hunt for, but I don't know

what's hunting for me.

The hunter becomes the hunted –

there are reasons I hunt I can't explain

like the way a falling leaf on a slight breeze speaks,

changes me.

The Deer in The Mist

. . . was more dream than real,

content to stay in a spot feeding

in that slow and still way deer have.

The mist stayed nearly an hour

and the hunter was nearly mesmerized

by those slow rhythms of movement

that teased the moment to be forever.

Then the sun broke through, slow but

burning the mist and the reality of the

deer became clearer and its size grew

into a precision beyond a deer in the mist.

The shot was made, the deer dropped.

The hunter paused,

caught by that moment where dream

had become reality.

It's hard to know which lingered more:

the dream or the shot.

Or if there was any difference.

Edge

I

The divine is a creature of the edge,

shadows or sign left behind are the preferred ways

of being known: if cornered, a dangerous thing.

The one who sees the divine with a naked eye

is never the same caught

between longing and having been satisfied.

I hunt deer,

know it's true.

the edges, the altars

of a sanctuary.

II

The divine is an edge creature.

Preferring not the projections of grandiosity

the congregation casts,

accepting those who see and hear

the meaning in silent shadows and ghostly flight

unable to know where one moment begins,

ends,

each caught in the other

the way deer appear

and disappear.

III

The divine is the creature of the edge.

It comes down to this: time elongated

by the woods and the heart,

the deer quietly, suddenly appears

and you unseen, take the shot,

blessing or cursing the moment.

"*The readiness is all*," whispered like a prayer

as you find out if you were ready or not –

the deer down, the deer not found,

the divine taken or escaping again.

Bow and Arrow

What the bow teaches is that certain things

all work together to hit the mark.

An equality of differences coordinated

in one act lets the heart, eye, and arrow see

one spot as if no other exists

and the release and follow through –

procession and recession –

commence and end nearly simultaneously.

Unless the art of holding and letting go

is not mastered then time shatters and eternity

splinters into infinity until the next time

when the arrow is put to the string,

laid on the rest, hand loosely to bow,

fingers to string,

eye and arrow

one and the same thing.

The Buck Appeared

First as a body of a deer

then the head showed the antlers.

Before he showed his head,

the body showed how large it was,

its sleek coat how healthy it was,

the shoulder muscles

and hindquarters how strong it was.

And then the antlers in that

powerful symmetry matched by that regal gait said,

"All other bucks leave when I am near."

He was not part of a group;

he was alone, unconcerned,

vigilant the way that kind of buck is.

He fed, flicked his tail contented,

disappeared the way deer do

right before your eyes.

From a Hundred Yards Away

. . . looking downhill I saw a buck,

at least a ten point with a body to match,

working a bush to get the velvet off his antlers.

I watched.

There

was nothing to do to get a shot;

besides, I didn't want to disrupt the scene

by pretending I could get closer

unseen.

The bush stopped moving,

the buck eased away in that cautionary,

careless step that speaks of something

I don't possess but know it when I see it.

He moved out of sight

and I walked slowly,

quietly down the hill to where

he had been, saw no deer after that.

Old Hunting Advice

I say, "follow the sign."

Wherever it takes you.

Especially when it takes you

where you don't want to go.

What you're looking for

and the expectations of how you'll find it

don't always match.

Are a better surprise when they don't.

Read the sign.

What you see in your mind's eye

and what you see

aren't likely to be the same.

Remember that.

I know I've looked for what I was looking for

and didn't see what was in front of me.

There's a blindness you have to be aware of.

The crazy thing is when I come out of the woods –

with or without game, I can't stop reading sign.

The urge *to see* and *to see into* doesn't leave me.

There.

That's all I know about

reading sign.

Hope it makes sense to you.

A Dream Remembered

I have long answered the call of the hunt

first heard in hunting stories,

embodied in maple bows I made

and cattail arrows with wooden carved arrowheads

and bird feathers for fletching.

Then I started to read

and reading led to acts

and acts to ignorance

and ignorance to knowledge

and knowledge to always the pursuit

of what both ignorance and knowledge give.

Lead to a love of the bow,

the synchronicity of the bow and me

that no squeezing of a cold steel trigger holds.

And the love of the woods

in an activity that promises no results,

the equation never the same.

But when there's a result, that ultimate result is

I always take out more than I've brought in –

a word, a phrase, a feeling,

a dream remembered,

a memory

not wanting to fade

that would not have occurred any place else —

I hunt.

A Place of Crossing, A Place of Ambush

I am awake before the deer are,

waking up slowly not like them,

like all wild creatures with that immediacy

of open eyes and heart and mind at-the-ready;

that is *all* more slowly done in me.

I see where I want to be in an hour or so,

a place of crossing,

a place of ambush,

a place where a bow can be drawn, shot released.

I think to how love and sorrow

have ambushed me,

how at some crossing,

some intersection

I have been most exposed to joy or sorrow

only to hear that flight of the arrow –

the mark, my heart, strike me unaware

I was being taken.

"You're hunting deer," I remind myself,

it's simply hunting,

the solemnity of a crossing,

the essence of an ambush,

just being both awake and silent enough

to know when a deer is coming.

Love and sorrow,

just this side of despair, is in the air.

I sip my coffee, look at the clock, think,

It's almost time to get ready.

The Promise of Deer in Late Summer

The promise of deer in late summer, early fall

remains though seeing them gets harder,

their willingness to be seen less true.

They have not yet hit the rut,

that recklessness that exposes bucks to hunters

in ways their summer sightings, early fall groupings

do not. I know there's no love involved

only that mad urge to procreate, to get to that state

of "*rutted out*," to fall back in exhaustion

to that cautionary life that bucks live in

most of their lives.

But that intense recklessness is something

I would possess, take like medicine in small doses,

to feel blood-gorged with a lust for life

in the wild confidence of doing what is mine

to do and then disappear safe

in some tangled underbrush

that can't be seen into.

Acknowledgements

Thank you, Tamarack Writers, who, for almost 50 years have helped me find the right words in the right order. More specifically, my express gratitude to author, friend and fellow Tamarack Writer David Daniel, whose laser focus feedback is matched only by his wit and insights. David's Foreword to this book vividly brings the perspective and balance of a non-hunter.

And a deep, heartfelt note of appreciation to fellow poet, outdoorsman and friend, Girard Tournesol who provided book cover design, editing, and publishing services for this book. Through his indie publishing company, Quimby, Pickford & Cheshire (named after his three dead cats), Girard provided highly motivating assistance getting this manuscript together in his role as my Executive Irritant.

To my beta readers, yet another dear Tamarack Writer Amy Farranto and personal friends Ray Bugay and Joanne Scheier, thank you for helping this old hunter's voice sound its best.

I'd also like to acknowledge my friend and former work colleague Christine Holt for her inspiration and contributions to the original chapbook *Meditations from a Tree Stand* which appears as Book 1 of this triptych.

And to all the friends, family and former colleagues on my Friday Poem email distribution list — thanks for being there with me all these years, listening, reading sign.

~ Byron Hoot, November 2022

About the Author

Byron Hoot was born into a family of ministers, raised in a minister's home and stayed in West Virginia until he went to college. The influence of church, his parents, the hymns, the sermons, the people, the questions raised and later answered on his life and literary work cannot be overstated.

Byron earned a BA from Nazarene colleges, a Master's in American Literature from West Virginia University, and accumulated course work for a PhD from the University of Maryland. He is previously married and has four children and five grandchildren. Although he long worked in the world of business, he is currently retired and lives "far from the maddening crowd."

He's hunted since his youth and fished for the last handful of years. Byron is as comfortable in the woods as he is reading poetry, sitting at a bar or sitting in church.

The woods have shaped him as much as anything else. His discipline is daily writing and reading for almost fifty years.

Byron's literary work has been published in Rattle, North/South Appalachia, Rye, Whisky Review, and The Pittsburgh Post-Gazette. His other books of poetry include *The Art of Grilling, In Our Time, Such Beautiful Sense* and *Piercing the Veil* with photographer Greg Clary.

Byron makes his home in The Pennsylvania Wilds region of Northern Appalachia.

Made in USA - North Chelmsford, MA
1345118_9798363051968
12.07.2022 0712